JOKES
Riddles
AND tongue
twisters

ARCTURUS

ARCTURUS

This edition published in 2017 by Arcturus Publishing Limited
26/27 Bickels Yard, 151–153 Bermondsey Street,
London SE1 3HA

ISBN: 978-1-78428-793-1
CH005584NT
Supplier 26, Date 0617, Print run 6209

Illustrated by Chuck Wheldon
Designed by Stefan Holliland
Edited by Samantha Hilton and Joe Harris

Printed in China

Contents

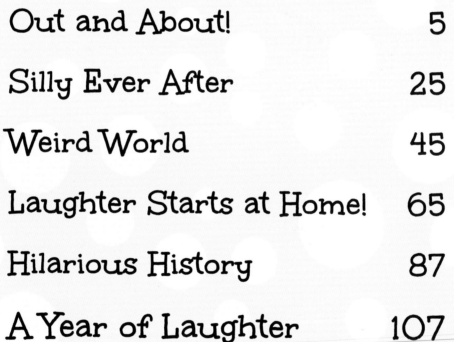

Out and About!   5

Silly Ever After   25

Weird World   45

Laughter Starts at Home!   65

Hilarious History   87

A Year of Laughter   107

Did you hear about the joke book that was covered in glue?

You couldn't put it down!

Don't worry, there's no glue in this one—well, hardly any...

4

Out and About!

What do you use to cut the ocean in two?

A seasaw!

Knock, knock.

Who's there?

Ken.

Ken who?

Ken I come in? It's freezing out here!

Where do sheep go on vacation?

The Baa-hamas!

What do you call a man with a car on his head?

Jack!

Riddle me this! I keep running and running, but I never get tired. What am I?

A river.

Why don't elephants travel by train?

They don't like putting their trunks on the luggage rack!

Which U.S. state is round at each end and high in the middle?

Ohio!

Try saying this three times, quickly.

She sells sea shells by the seashore!

What's brown, hairy, and wears sunglasses?

A coconut at the beach!

Riddle me this!

I fall at the North Pole, but I never get hurt. What am I?

Snow.

What are the only notes a pirate can sing?

High Cs!

Did you hear about the ship carrying blue paint that crashed into a ship carrying red paint?

The crews were marooned!

What vegetable do sailors hate? Leeks!

Knock, knock.

Who's there?

Canoe.

Canoe who?

Canoe come out and play?

Did you hear about the commuter who chewed gum every morning?

He caught the chew-chew train!

Try saying this three times, quickly.

The lucky crook took the cook's truck!

Why did the pirate give his ship a coat of paint?

Because its timbers were shivering!

How do lighthouse keepers communicate with each other?

With shine language!

What part of a car is the laziest?

The wheels, because they're always tired!

What do you get if you cross a dog and a plane

A jet-setter!

I'll only go to work after you've fired me. What am I?

A rocket!

What did the toad say to the hitchhiking frog?

Hop in!

What did the sea captain say to the pilot after takeoff?

This is plane sailing!

What did the sailor think as he fell overboard?

Water way to go!

How do you annoy a pirate? Take away the "p" to make him irate!

Where do sharks go for a weekend break? Fin-land!

Try saying this three times, quickly.

Can a toucan canoe in the Yukon?

When is a car like a frog? When it's being toad!

Why did the spy get arrested at the station? He was trying to cover his tracks!

Which U.S. state sneezes the most? Mass-achoo-setts!

Why did the sailor cross the road?

To get to the other tide!

Why is it hard to find a camel in the desert?

Because they're well camel-flaged!

What do you call a sleepy bull?

A bulldozer!

Did you hear about the sick bicycle?

It was bed-ridden!

Riddle me this!

I jump when I walk and sit when I stand. What am I?

A kangaroo.

Why did the pirate leave a chicken with his buried treasure?

Because eggs marks the spot!

What is fluffy and green? A seasick sheep!

Why couldn't the astronaut land on the moon? Because it was full!

What do you call a pirate with three eyes? A piiirate!

How do you throw a space party? You planet!

How did the hairdresser win the cycle race? She took a shortcut!

Try saying this three times, quickly.
Jumping jaguars juggle in the jungle!

How do pirates communicate with each other?

They use "Aye, aye!" phones!

Riddle me this! I'm not a tree, but I grow branches on my head. What am I?

A deer.

What's fruity and purple and found off the coast of Australia?

The Grape Barrier Reef!

If there are ten cats on a train and one gets off, how many are left?

None—they're all copycats!

What shoes should you wear when taking the train?

Platform shoes!

Did you hear about the frog that parked illegally?

It got toad away!

How do elephants travel long distances? In jumbo jets!

What do sailors like in their soup?

Crew-tons!

What is the hardest thing when you learn to ride a bike?

The ground!

Riddle me this! This key opens no doors, but you'll find it swinging through the jungle. What is it?

A monkey.

What do you call a parrot that lives in a Mercedes?

A flying car-pet!

What do you call a Frenchman wearing sandals?

Phillipe Flop!

What is big, round, furry, and flies?

A hot-air baboon!

What do you get if you meet a shark in the Arctic Ocean?

Frostbite!

Say this three times, quickly.

The sixth sick sailor sat in the sinking ship!

Riddle me this!

I'm a type of building, but I weigh very little. What am I?

A lighthouse.

Why did the snake cross the desert?

To get to the other sssssside!

What has big ears, four legs, and a trunk?

A mouse with its luggage.

What do you call a camel without a hump?

Humphrey!

Why do seagulls live by the sea?

Because if they lived by the bay, they'd be bagels!

Can you name five animals found at the North Pole?

Four seals and a polar bear!

What did the four-by-four owner say in the blizzard?

"Snow problem!"

What's big, scary, and has three wheels?

A T. rex riding a tricycle!

Which animal was the first in space?

The cow who jumped over the Moon!

Where do pencils come from?

Pencil-vania!

How do engines hear?

Through their engine-ears!

Why should you never argue on a hot-air balloon ride?

You don't want to fall out!

Which is the fastest country in the world?

Rush-a!

Riddle me this! What do maps, fish, and music all have in common?

Scales.

How do fleas travel from place to place?

They itch-hike!

What do you call the streams that flow into the Nile?

Juveniles!

Say this three times, quickly.

It's terrifically tricky to trap twin tigers!

What do spiders study at art school?

Web design!

When is a sailor like a plank of wood?

When he's aboard!

Knock, knock.
Who's there?
Mandy.
Mandy who?
Man, de traffic is terrible tonight!

Where do cows spend the night when they're away from home?

A moo-tel!

What snakes do you find on cars?

Windshield vipers!

Why do bananas use sunscreen?

Because they peel!

Knock, knock!

Who's there?

Joanna.

Joanna who?

Joanna go for a walk with me?

Which country is full of giant sea creatures?

Wales!

Why are maps so bad at poker?

Because they always fold!

Who earns a living by driving their customers away?

A cab driver!

What's heavy, smelly, has four wheels, and flies?

A garbage truck on a hot summer's day!

What do you call a train with a cold?

An achoo-choo train!

What do you call a boomerang that doesn't come back?

A stick!

What flower is like a country of automobiles?

A car-nation!

What kind of hairstyle do sailors have?

A crew cut!

You will find me in the middle of nowhere. What am I?

The letter "h"!

What did one flag say to the other?

Nothing, it just waved!

What is the best day to go the beach?

Sun-day!

Why do ghosts visit the same places every year?

They like their old haunts best!

How do you get ice off a hot-air balloon?

Use a skyscraper!

Did you hear the joke about the little mountain?

It's hill-arious!

Say this three times, quickly.

The ten-ton train rattles through the tunnel!

What do you call a man that blocks a river?

Adam!

What did the baby bicycle call its father?

Pop-cycle!

Which is the coldest country in the world?

Chile!

What should you take to avoid seasickness?

Vitamin sea!

How do bees get to school?

They take the school buzz!

What did the fish say when it swam into the concrete wall?

"Dam!"

What does a houseboat want to be when it grows up?

A township!

I am the strongest animal under the sea. What am I?

A mussel!

Where do sailors keep their books?

On the continental shelf!

Why did the pirate visit the Apple store?

To buy an i-Patch!

Why did the farmer ride his horse into town?

Because it was too heavy to carry!

Where do hamsters come from?

Hamsterdam!

What do Inuit people use to hold their houses together?

Ig-glue!

If shoes are made from leather, what's made from bananas?

Slippers!

Why do French people love to eat snails?

They don't like fast food!

Why did the bridge get angry?

Because people were always crossing it!

Riddle me this! **A man went into town on Friday, stayed two nights, then went home on Friday. How?**

His horse's name was Friday!

What goes MOOZ?

A spaceship reversing!

What's worse than raining cats and dogs?

Hailing taxis!

What do you need to drive your car underwater?

Four-eel drive!

What kind of music do astronauts like?

Rocket and roll!

Why did the robot go on vacation?

He needed to recharge his batteries!

Did you hear about the cuddly sea captain?

He liked to hug the shore!

Riddle me this! I live in the sea, but I look like I'm from outer space. What am I?

A starfish.

What was the highest mountain before Everest was discovered?

Still Mount Everest!

Say this three times, quickly.

The ship's chef's sushi made Suzie seasick!

Silly Ever After

Why don't bad-tempered witches ride broomsticks?

In case they fly off the handle!

What happened to the wizard who skipped school?

He was ex-spelled!

Why did Little Miss Muffet need a map?

Because she'd lost her whey!

Try saying this three times, quickly.

This witch wishes to switch wands!

Why should you never sleep with your head under the pillow?

Because the tooth fairy might take all your teeth!

Did you hear about the witches who were identical twins?

You couldn't tell which witch was which!

Why do dragons lay eggs?

Because if they dropped them, they would break!

What do sea monsters eat?

Fish and ships!

Try saying this quickly, three times!

If two witches were watching two watches, which witch would watch which watch?

What did the mermaid keep as a pet?

A catfish!

What's the first thing a witch reads in a magazine?

Her horror-scope!

Riddle me this!

I magically turn everything around without touching anything at all. What am I?

A mirror.

Why was Cinderella thrown off the football team?

Because she kept running away from the ball!

Try saying this quickly, three times.

Glowing, green globes glisten in the gloom.

Which North American lake is popular with witches?

Lake Eerie!

What does a wizard put on his hair?

Scare gel!

Why don't witches wear top hats?

Because there's no point!

Why did the mermaid blush? Because she saw the bottom of the ocean!

Who keeps the ocean floor clean?

The mermaids!

Did you hear about the wizard who turned himself into a frog?

He's still hopping mad about it!

Try saying this three times, quickly.

Dwayne the dwarf drew Dracula's weird dragon!

Knock, knock.

Who's there?

Witches.

Witches who?

Witches the way to the Monster's Ball?

What do you get when you cross a witch with a dinosaur?

A Tyrannosaurus hex!

Where do ogres like to go shopping?

The gross-ery store!

Riddle me this! What has a head and a tail but no body?

A coin.

Knock, knock.
Who's there?
Ivana.
Ivana who?
Ivana suck your blood!

Did you hear about the vampire who loved baseball?

He kept turning into a bat!

What did the witch say to the black cat?

You seem familiar!

What did the fairy name her daughter?

Wanda!

Why didn't the mermaid warn her daughter about the electric eel?

It was too shocking!

Why was the Genie of the Lamp so grumpy?

Someone had rubbed him up the wrong way!

What do you say when you meet a werewolf?

"Howl do you do?"

Why did the silly boy carry a cuckoo clock on Halloween?

He'd heard it was tick or tweet!

How does an octopus make a mermaid laugh?

With ten-tickles!

Why do witches love hotels?

They can order broom service!

What is a witch's best subject at school?

Spelling!

Riddle me this! I have a face and two hands but no arms or legs. What am I?

A clock.

Knock, knock.

Who's there?

Ice cream.

Ice cream who?

Ice cream if you don't let me in!

Why was the witch late for school?

Because she overswept!

What's the difference between a unicorn and a carrot?

One is a funny beast, and the other is a bunny feast!

Try saying this three times, quickly.

Trixie picks pink pansies for pixies!

What does Cinderella wear underwater?

Glass flippers!

Why didn't the pixie invite his school friend over for supper?

His mother couldn't stand the goblin!

How do you make a witch itch?

Take away the "w"!

What do you give an ogre with enormous feet?

Plenty of room!

What type of dog does dracula have?

A bloodhound!

What do you call a petunia that goes to magic school?

Harry Potplant!

Riddle me this!

I have thirteen hearts but no brains. What am I?

A deck of cards.

How does an ogre count to twelve?

On his fingers!

Where do witches leave their children while they're at work?

Dayscare!

What do ghosts like to eat for dessert?

I scream!

Try saying this three times, quickly!

The cute Quidditch kids quit the Quidditch pitch quite quietly.

Why does Peter Pan fly everywhere?

He Neverlands!

How do you know when a magician has lost his temper?

He pulls his hare out!

What is taller than a giant?

A giant's hat!

Where do you find giant snails?

On a giant's fingers!

Did you hear about the ugly Cyclops?

He was a sight for a sore eye!

Try saying this three times, quickly.

Gargling gargoyles gobble gross goblins greedily!

Knock, knock.

Who's there?

Ogre.

Ogre who?

O gr-eat, you're at home!

Who goes out with an ogre?

His girlfiend!

34

What kind of books do magician's rabbits like?

Ones with hoppy endings!

Why did the wizard fail his exam?

He was terrible at spelling!

How do mermaids like their hair?

Wavy!

Why aren't vampires very good at art?

Because they can only draw blood!

What did the skeleton order for dinner?

Spare ribs!

Try saying this three times, quickly.

The wizard winked wickedly while waving his wand!

What do you call a wizard from outer space?

A flying sorcerer!

What kind of witch is useful when it's dark?

A lights-witch!

Say this three times, quickly.

The green goblins greedily gobbled their gooey goodies!

Why did Dopey the dwarf stare at the orange juice carton for hours?

Because the label said "Concentrate"!

Why did the octopus annoy the mermaid?

He was always squidding around!

What stories did Goldilocks tell the three bears?

Furry tales!

Who is Aladdin's smartest friend?

The genie-us of the lamp!

Knock, knock.

Who's there?

Tinker bell.

Tinker bell who?

I tinker bell is out of order!

How do mermaids do their shopping?

They surf the net!

What position does a ghost play in soccer?

Ghoulie!

Where do you find giant armies?

In a giant's sleevies!

Knock, knock.

Who's there?

Frank.

Frank who?

Frankenstein!

What do you call a skeleton who won't work?

Lazy bones!

Why should you never trust the big bad wolf when he's in bed?

Because he's lying!

Where do the toughest dragons come from?

Hard-boiled eggs!

What do witches always eat at Halloween?

Ghoulash!

Why didn't the mummy have any friends?

Because he was too wrapped up in himself!

Why did the skeleton stay at home?

Because he had no body to go out with!

Say this three times, quickly.

Eleven elves ate enchanted eggs in an elm tree!

What fruit do ghosts like best?

Boo-berries!

What do French skeletons say before dinner?

Bone appetit!

Riddle me this!

How do you make the number one disappear?

Add the letter "G" and it's "GONE"!

What game do vampires love to play?

Casket-ball!

What is at the end of a rainbow?

The letter "w"!

What do you get if you take a bunch of witches to the beach?

A pile of sand-witches!

What has a blue face and a horn on its head?

A unicorn holding its breath!

Where does Count Dracula keep his money?

In a blood bank!

Why don't ghosts like the rain?

It dampens their spirits!

Why are ghosts so bad at lying?

Because you can see right through them!

What do vampires do at the end of the school year?

Blood tests!

Riddle me this!

I have an eye, but I cannot see. What am I?

A needle.

How did Jack figure out how many beans his cow was worth?

He used a cow-culator!

What do you call a one-eyed creature riding a BMX?

A bicyclops!

Say this three times, quickly. **Sixty pesky pixies pestered poor Peter!**

Did you hear about the magician that threw his watch up in the air?

He wanted to see time fly!

Why do witches fly on brooms?

Because vacuum cleaners are too heavy!

What's purple and screams from the top of a tower?

A damson in distress!

Riddle me this! **You'll never see us by daylight, although there are billions of us. What are we?**

Stars.

What do you call a creature that gets lost when there's a full moon?

A where-wolf!

What do you do with a green monster?

Wait until it's ripe!

Knock, knock.

Who's there?

Jacklyn.

Jacklyn who?

Jacklyn Hyde!

Why don't bats live alone?

They like hanging out with their friends!

What do witches spread on their bread?

Scream cheese!

Did you hear the gloomy story about the bear?

It was a grim, furry tale!

Riddle me this!
Just one shade but changing size. Present in sunlight but gone at night! What am I?
A shadow.

What happened when two banshees met each other at a party?
It was love at first fright!

Why doesn't Harry Potter's godfather like practical jokes?
He's always Sirius!

Why didn't the zombie go to school?
Because he felt rotten!

Say this three times, quickly.
Which wicked witch wished the wicked wish?

How can you tell if a banshee is polite?
She only shrieks when she's spoken to!

What is the first thing pixies learn at school?

The elf-abet!

Why can't you borrow money from a leprechaun?

They're always a a little short!

Knock, knock.

Who's there?

Fifi.

Fifi who?

Fifi, fiefie, fofo, fum, I smell the blood of an Englishman!

Why do dragons sleep during the day?

So they can fight knights!

How do we know Rapunzel liked to party?

Because she always let her hair down!

What has sharp teeth and lives at the end of the rainbow?

The croc of gold!

Weird World

Did you hear about the snakes that argued?

They agreed to hiss and make up!

What did the tornado say to the plane?

"Want to go for a spin?"

How do snails keep their shells so shiny?

They use snail polish!

What did the cloud say to the bolt of lightning?

"You're shocking!"

What do you call a funny chicken?

A comedi-hen!

A pony went to see the doctor because it had a sore throat. "I know what's wrong," said the doctor. "You're a little horse!"

What part of the ocean is the deepest?

The bottom!

Why couldn't the snake say anything?

It had a frog in its throat!

What did the worm say to her son when he came home late?

"Where in earth have you been?"

Where do fish keep their money?

In the riverbank!

What kind of clothes do storm clouds wear?

Thunderwear!

How can you tell that a cat likes the rain?

Because when it rains, it purrs!

Riddle me this!

I often drop, but I never hit the ground. What am I?

The temperature.

What is on top of a snowman's bed?

A blanket of snow!

Why aren't trees good at quizzes?

Because they're often stumped!

Did you hear about the silkworms that had a race?

They ended up in a tie!

What do horses wear at the beach?

Clip-clops!

Riddle me this! What is the largest moth in the world? A mammoth.

What do cows do when they visit New York? They go to see a moosical!

Why is it hard to tease a snake? You can't pull its leg!

What dog loves to take bubble baths? A shampoodle!

What's black and white and red all over? A sunburned penguin!

What kind of tree can fit into your hand? A palm tree!

What musical instrument are fish afraid of?

Casta-nets!

Did you hear about the bee born in the spring?

Maybee...

Why do trees hate exams?

They are easily stumped!

Knock, knock.
Who's there?
Cowsgo.
Cowsgo who?
No, they don't.
Cows go moo!

Why shouldn't you tell jokes in the Arctic?

The ice might crack up!

Try saying this three times, quickly.

Six silver swans swam silently seaward!

Why do male deer need to wear braces?

Because they have buck teeth!

What did the duck say after he went shopping?

Put it on my bill!

Which animals are caterpillars most afraid of?

Dog-erpillars!

This animal wears a coat in winter, but in summer, it wears a coat and pants. What is it?

A dog!

Why don't oysters share their pearls?

Because they're shellfish!

Which sea creature eats its prey two at a time?

Noah's shark!

Why don't oysters like loud music?
Because a noisy noise annoys an oyster!

What did the vet give the sick horse?
Cough stirrup!

Why do penguins carry fish in their beaks?
Because they don't have any pockets!

Say this three times, quickly.
I think extinct insects stink!

What kind of pigs know karate?
Pork chops!

What's worse than finding a worm in your apple?
Finding half a worm in your apple!

What do you call a mackerel in a tuxedo?

So-fish-ticated!

Say this three times, quickly.

The six, sick slimy snails sailed silently!

What do you call a snake that works for the government?

A civil serpent!

What do you call an ambitious wasp?

A wanna-bee!

What happened to the snowman in the spring?

He made a pool of himself!

What game do tornadoes play?

Twister!

What sound do porcupines make when they kiss?

Ouch!

Say this three times, quickly.

A big, black bug blew big, blue bubbles!

Why are dolphins so clever?

Because they swim in schools!

What do acorns learn at school?

Their tree times table!

What do you call a deer with no eyes?

No idea!

What did the crab say to her grouchy husband?

"Don't get snappy with me!"

What do polar bears eat for lunch?
Iceberg-ers!

Why does the Moon wear sunglasses?
Because it's way cooler than the Sun!

Say this three times, quickly.
If you go for a gopher, the gopher will go for a hole!

What do you call a baby crab?
A little nipper!

Why wasn't the octopus afraid of being attacked?
It was well armed!

What did one raindrop say to the other?
"Two's company, three's a cloud!"

How do you stop a rhino from charging?
Unplug it!

Why don't owls date during thunderstorms?
It's too wet to woo!

Say this three times, quickly.

How much wood would a woodchuck chuck, if a woodchuck could chuck wood?

Riddle me this!

Go ahead and slice me apart ... you'll be the one crying! What am I?

An onion.

Why can't a leopard hide?

Because he's always spotted!

What's the best season to buy a trampoline?

Spring!

How do you get rid of an annoying wasp?

Tell it to buzz off!

What lives in the forest and never stops talking?

A wild boar!

What does the Sun drink out of?
Sunglasses!

What is in the middle of a jellyfish?
Its jelly button!

Why did the Sun go to school?
To get brighter!

Try saying this three times, quickly.
Felix fries fresh fish for Friday's fresh-fish festival!

Knock, knock.
Who's there?
Toucan.
Toucan who?
Toucan play that game!

What is the biggest ant in the world?
The eleph-ant!

What kind of animal is the best at breakdancing?

A hip-hop-potamus!

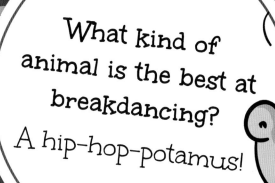

What do you get if you cross a frog with a flower?

A croak-us!

Did you hear about the happy raindrop?

It was on Cloud Nine!

Say this three times, quickly.

Swedish sword-swallowers swallow swords swiftly!

What do you call a woman who is good at fishing?

Annette!

What is a snake's best subject?

Hiss-tory!

Knock, knock.

Who's there?

Rhino.

Rhino who?

Rhino every knock, knock joke there is!

What do trees wear to the pool?

Swimming trunks!

Why don't fish ever win at poker?

Because of all the card sharks!

What do you call a bee that keeps falling over?

A stumble-bee!

How do you describe an acorn?

In a nutshell, it's an oak tree!

What are the silliest flowers in the garden?

Daffy-dils!

What did the tree do when the bank was closed?

It tried another branch!

What did the bird say as it finished building its nest?

"That's the last straw!"

What do you call a rabbit with fleas?

Bugs bunny!

What do you call a bee that is unhappy?

A grumble-bee!

Riddle me this!

I'm an insect, and the first half of my name is another insect. What am I?

A beetle.

What do you call a man with pockets full of dry leaves?

Russell!

Riddle me this!
Feed me and I live, but give me a drink, and I die. What am I?
Fire.

Knock, knock.
Who's there?
Bat.
Bat who?
Bat you'll never guess!

What do you call a man with a seagull on his head?
Cliff!

What should you do in the presence of a mighty tree?
Take a bough!

What do you call a snake that builds houses?
A boa constructor!

How do you get in touch with a fish?
You drop it a line!

Why didn't the viper wipe 'er nose?

Because the adder 'ad 'er 'andkerchief!

Which animal can jump higher than a building?

All animals can ... because buildings can't jump!

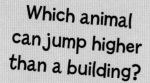

Why do you call that reptile "Tiny"?

Because he's my newt!

What do you get from a pampered cow?

Spoiled milk!

What is a myth?

A female moth!

Say this three times, quickly.

Two tiny tigers took taxis into town!

What does a lion say when he's introduced at a party?

Pleased to eat you!

What do you call a girl with a turtle on her head?

Shelley!

What did the farmer say to the cow when she ran out of milk?

You're an udder failure!

What's orange and sounds like a parrot?

A carrot!

Riddle me this! I am most useful when I'm broken. What am I?

An egg.

Cindy: It's really raining cats and dogs today.

Mindy: I know, I just stepped in a poodle!

What month do lumberjacks like the best?

Sep-timber!

Say this three times, quickly.

How many clams can you cram in a clean cream can?

What do you call a sheep with no legs?

A cloud!

Who stole the soap?

The robber ducky!

What's full of holes but holds lots of water?

A sponge!

What do you call a bear in wet weather?

A drizzly bear!

How can you tell a worm's head from its tail?

Tickle the middle, and see which end laughs!

What game did the cat like to play with the mouse?

Catch!

Say this three times, quickly.

Can a toucan do the cancan? Can two toucans do the cancan, too?

What do you call a T. rex with magical powers?

A dino-sorcerer!

What type of bird works on a building site?

A crane!

No matter how much it rains, I never get any wetter. What am I?

A lake.

Laughter Starts at Home!

Mother: Please can you help me fix dinner?

Daughter: Why, is it broken?

Why was the octopus worried about her son?

Because he was a crazy, mixed-up squid!

Riddle me this!

I'm tall when I'm young but short when I'm old. What am I?

A candle.

Did you hear that Uncle Bob lost his wig on the roller coaster?

It was a hair-raising experience!

Kurt: What has four legs, pimples, and smells bad?

Bert: Me and my brother!

Riddle me this!

What goes up but never comes down?

Your age.

Dad: **Why have you been missing school, son?**

Son: I haven't missed it one little bit!

What did the mother dog say to the puppy?

"We're having dinner soon ... don't eat too much homework!"

Why did the woman go out of the house with her purse open?

She expected some change in the weather!

Say this three times, quickly.

Simon's sister's socks sat in a sink soaking in soapsuds!

Emily: **Dad, I got an A in spelling!**

Dad: You fool, there isn't an "A" in "spelling"!

Raquel: Why does your dad wear two sweaters when he plays golf?

Michelle: In case he gets a hole in one!

What did the mother broom say to her son at bedtime?

"It's time to go to sweep!"

What do you get if you cross Dad's socks with a boomerang?

A nasty smell that keeps coming back!

What do you get if you cross baked beans with onions?

Tear gas!

How do you define "cartoon"?

Music you listen to in the car!

Knock, knock.

Who's there?

Anita.

Anita who?

Anita borrow a cup of sugar!

Do robots have brothers?
No, but they do have transistors!

What do you do if you find a dinosaur in your bed?
Find somewhere else to sleep!

Why was the little iceberg just like his dad?
Because he was a chip off the cold block!

Knock, knock.
Who's there?
Dishes
Dishes who?
Dish-es me, who are you?

Which fruit do twins like best?
Pears!

What can you give and keep at the same time?
A cold!

Winnie: Why is there a plane outside your bedroom door?

Vinnie: I must have left the landing light on!

My cousin is so dumb, he took his computer to the nurse because it had a virus!

What did the Italian say when he returned from an overseas trip?

"Rome, sweet Rome!"

Say this three times, quickly.

If your dog chews shoes, whose shoes does he choose?

David's father has three sons: Snap, Crackle, and...?

David!

What kind of monster lives in your brother's room?

The Loch Mess Monster!

Why did the boy throw butter out of the window?

To see the butterfly!

My mother's excellent at history, but she's an awful cook.

She's an expert on ancient grease!

Why is your sister so good at sports?

She has athlete's foot!

Say this three times, quickly.

There's a kitten in mittens eating chicken in the kitchen!

Why were the glowworms' parents so happy?

Because their children were all very bright!

Dad: There's a burglar downstairs eating the cake Aunt Agatha baked.

Daughter: Should I call the police or an ambulance?

What is stranger than seeing a cat fish?

Seeing a goldfish bowl!

Kid: Can I have a canary for Christmas?

Dad: No, you'll have turkey, like everyone else!

Daughter: I can't mow the lawn today. I've twisted my ankle.

Mother: That's a lame excuse!

Why was the youngest of seven children late for school?

Because the alarm was set for six!

Knock, knock.

Who's there?

Aunt.

Aunt who?

Aunt you gonna let me in?

What do you call a baby skunk?

A little squirt!

Why did the cat always hang out near the piano?
She was looking for the piano tuna!

Why did the house go to the hospital?
Because it had a windowpane!

What should you do if a teenage monster rolls her eyes at you?
Roll them back to her!

Say this three times, quickly.
Will merry Murray marry Mary or Marie?

Knock, knock.
Who's there?
Someone on a pogo stick.
Tell them to hop it!

What did the baby corn say to his mother?
Where's Pop?

What do you give to a baby snake?

A rattle!

I am a room with no walls. What am I?

A mushroom.

Knock, knock.
Who's there?
Lettuce.
Lettuce who?
Lettuce in! We're freezing!

When should a mouse stay indoors?

When it's raining cats and dogs!

Why shouldn't you worry if you see mice in your home?

They're probably doing the mouse-work!

What do you say to someone sitting on your roof?

"High there!"

Say this three times, quickly.

I like a proper cup of coffee from a proper copper coffee pot!

"Son, why didn't you come straight home from school?"

"Because we live around the corner!"

Son: This fish has bones in it.
Mother: Are you choking?
Son: No, I'm serious!

Sean: Why does your dog wear gloves?
Vaughn: It's a boxer!

"My dad had to go to court for stealing a calendar. You know what he got?"

"Twelve months!"

What Ancient Greek land is like your brother's bedroom?

Mess-opotamia!

Why are there more ghost cats than ghost dogs?

Because every cat has nine lives!

"Why is your brother running around his bed?"

"He's trying to catch up on his sleep!"

When is a basketball player like a baby?

When he dribbles!

What did the quilt say to the bed?

"I've got you covered!"

"Did your mother help you with your homework?"

"No, I got it wrong all by myself!"

What has many keys but cannot open a door?

A piano.

Thelma: If that planet is Mars, what's the one higher up?

Velma: Is it Pa's?

When is a door not a door?
When it's a jar!

Who are small, furry, and fantastic at sword fighting?
The Three Mouseketeers!

What happened when Granny Smith married Mr. Braeburn?
They lived appley ever after!

What happened when the invisible man married the invisible woman?
Their kids were nothing to look at!

Why is your dog chasing its tail?
It's trying to make both ends meet!

Why are you eating that baguette in the bathtub?

It's a sub sandwich!

Did you hear about the embarrassing dads in the fathers' race?

One ran in short bursts, the other ran in burst shorts!

Knock, knock.
Who's there?
Little old lady.
Little old lady who?
Wow! I didn't know you could yodel!

What prize did the inventor of the door knocker win?

The No-bell Prize!

What instrument do dogs like best?

The trom-bone!

Edwin: I don't like cheese with holes.

Dad: Well, eat the cheese, and leave the holes on the side of your plate!

What did one toilet say to the other?

"You look flushed!"

Knock, knock.
Who's there?
Amit.
Amit who?
Amit your sister at the movies last night!

How do you know when there's an elephant under your bed?

Your nose is touching the ceiling!

Riddle me this!
What belongs to you, even though other people use it more than you do?

Your name.

How do you warm up a room after it's been painted?

Give it a second coat!

How do you make antifreeze?

Hide her coat and gloves!

My brother is so dumb, he found three milk cartons in a field and thought it was a cow's nest!

Why did the robber take a bath before he stole from the bank?

He wanted to make a clean getaway!

I am as light as a feather, but no one can hold me for long. What am I?

Your breath.

What do you give your pet rat to eat?

Ratatouille!

"Dad, how can I join the police?"

"Handcuff them all together!"

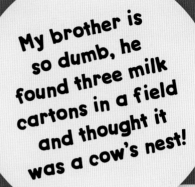

What happened to the dog that swallowed a firefly?

Its spark was worse than its bite!

Teacher: What is the plural of baby?

Frances: Twins!

What do a pet dog and a phone have in common?

They both have collar I.D.!

Say this three times, quickly.

These tricky tongue twisters trip thrillingly off the tongue!

Why did the programmer sell his cat?

He thought it might eat his mouse!

Why do dogs run in circles?

Because it's hard to run in squares!

Why did the police officer arrest his cat?

He saw the kitty litter!

What did the mother cow say to her calf at night?

"It's pasture bedtime!"

Why was the baby panda so spoiled? Because its mother panda-d to its every whim!

Why did the jogger eat on the run? She loved fast food!

I go up and down but never move. What am I? Stairs.

Annie: Why did your dad quit his job at the can-crushing plant?"

Danny: Because it was soda pressing!

Riddle me this!

What goes up when the rain comes down?

An umbrella.

Why are an old man's teeth like stars?

Because they come out at night!

Why is the letter "A" most like a flower?

Because the "B" is after it!

What do you call cheese that isn't yours?

Nacho cheese!

Why was the cat silent?

A person got its tongue!

How do you know carrots are good for your eyes?

Because you never see a rabbit wearing glasses!

What do cats put in their cola?

Mice cubes!

What did the cowboy say when his pet dog ran away?

"Well, doggone!"

Sandy: Can we watch The Curse of the Black Pearl tonight?

Mandy: No, Dad won't let us watch pirate DVDs!

How did the dog feel after he ate the pillow?

Down in the mouth!

Ron: Why are you taking planks and a hammer to the gym?

John: I'm going for fencing lessons!

What book do sharks read to their kids at bedtime?

Huckleberry Fin!

Which relative visits astronauts in outer space?

Auntie Gravity!

What's the difference between a moaning parent and a boring book?

You can shut a book up!

Dan: My teacher says I should train to be an astronaut.

Anne: No, he said you're a real space cadet!

Why was 6 scared of 7?

Because 7, 8, 9!

What does a fashionable house wear?

Address!

Spike: My dog's got no nose!

Mike: How does he smell?

Spike: Terrible!

Why did the mushroom get invited to so many parties?

Because he was a fun guy!

Why did the students eat their homework?

Because the teacher said that it was a piece of cake!

What makes you say your brother is dumb?

He tried to borrow Facebook from the library!

What time is it when an elephant sits on your fence?

Time to get a new fence!

Little pencil: You look as though you've put on weight, Dad.

Daddy pencil: You're very blunt!

Did you hear about the cat that swallowed a ball of yarn?

She had mittens!

Knock, Knock.
Who's there?
Cash.
Cash who?
I knew you were a nut!

How can you spell something rotten with just two letters?
D.K.!

My dad can juggle eggshells, yesterday's newspaper, and an empty box!
That's garbage!

Did you hear about the magician who tried his sawing-a-person-in-two tricks at home?
He had lots of half brothers and sisters!

Riddle me this!
I have one foot, one head, and four legs.
What am I?
A bed.

How many skunks does it take to stink up a house?
A phew!

Hilarious History

What was the first thing said by the inventor of the stink bomb?

"You reek, ugh!"

Where did Montezuma go to college?

Az Tech!

Say this three times, quickly.

Two terrible T. rex wreck trains together!

Who succeeded the first President of the United States?

The second one!

What do you call a sleeping Triceratops?

A dino-snore!

Who built the ark?

I have Noah idea!

Why did Eve want to move to New York?

She wanted to see the Big Apple!

Why were the early days of history called the Dark Ages?

Because there were so many knights!

Which king invented fractions?

Henry the $\frac{1}{8}$!

What was Camelot famous for?

Its knight life!

How did Vikings send secret messages?

They used Norse code!

How do you find Tutankhamen's tomb?

Peer-amid the other tombs!

Which ancient people moved around the most?

The Roam-ans!

Why does the Statue of Liberty stand outside New York?

It can't sit down!

What invention lets you see through walls?

The window!

Need an ark to save two of every animal?

I Noah guy...

Which cat discovered America?

Christofur Columpuss!

What do you call a Roman emperor with a cold?

Julius Sneezer!

What were Julius Sneezer's dying words?

"Achoo, Brute!"

Why did Renoir become an Impressionist?

He did it for the Monet!

What movie did the ancient Greeks like best?

Troy Story!

Say this three times, quickly.

Tutankhamun tucked twenty treasures in his tomb!

Why did everyone in nineteenth-century England carry an umbrella?

Because Queen Victoria's reign lasted for 64 years!

What do you call a dinosaur with no eyes?

Doyouthinkhesaurus!

Which famous gunfighter had indigestion?

Wyatt Burp!

Who was Wyatt Burp's best friend?

Wild Bill Hiccup!

What happened to the royal chicken that couldn't lay eggs?

The king had her eggs-ecuted!

Why can't you hear a Pterodactyl going to the bathroom?

Because the "p" is silent!

Did you hear about the card game on Noah's Ark?

It was ruined by a cheetah!

Which owl robbed the rich to give to the poor?

Robin Hoot!

What do history teachers talk about on dates?

The good old days!

How was the Roman empire divided?

With a pair of Caesars!

Who made King Arthur's round table?

Sir Cumference!

What is the fruitiest subject at school?

History, because it's full of dates!

What kind of king wears a horned crown?

A Vi-king!

Which figure in history ate the most?
Attila the Hungry!

What happened when electricity was first discovered?
People got a nasty shock!

Which Russian leader was a big fan of fruit?
Peter the Grape!

Say this three times, quickly.
Cunning Cleopatra's clever scheming charmed Caesar!

Why were the ancient Egyptians so unhappy with their ruler?
Because he was being un-Pharaoh!

What do kings and queens drink at breakfast?
Royal-tea!

Why were the ancient Egyptians good at spying?

They kept things under wraps!

What was written on the knight's tomb?

"Rust in Peace"!

Why was the ancient Egyptian mummy so tense?

He was always wound up!

Knock, knock.

Who's there?

Robin.

Robin who?

Robin the rich to give to the poor!

Which emperor should have stayed away from gunpowder?

Napoleon Blownapart!

What do you call a fortunate detective?

Sheerluck Holmes!

How did pharaohs get the best pyramids?

They asked for a tomb with a view!

Say this three times, quickly.

Sly pirates spy pilots buying pies!

What was Robin Hood's mother called?

Mother Hood!

What is a forum?

Two-um plus two-um!

Which monarch had the worst skin?

Mary, Queen of Spots!

What do you call a frog who wants to be a cowboy?

Hop-along Cassidy!

Why did the student miss the history exam?

He had the wrong date!

Where did King Arthur's men get their training?

Knight school!

Was Rome built in a day?

No, it was built in Italy!

Which famous explorer was good at sports?

Marco Polo!

Did you hear about the unembalmed ancient Egyptian discovery?

It sphinx!

What happened when the wheel was invented?

It started a revolution!

Why did cavemen love to eat sloths?

They knew that fast food was bad for you!

Why did Robin Hood only steal from the rich?

Because the poor had nothing worth stealing!

Where was the Declaration of Independence signed?

At the bottom!

Why was King Arthur's table round?

So he couldn't be cornered!

Try saying this three times, quickly.

Upon the placid plains, the Pawnee ponies pranced!

When in history did people have the nicest, smoothest clothes?

During the Iron Age!

Which fruit launched a thousand ships?

Melon of Troy!

What did Henry VIII do whenever he burped?

He issued a Royal Pardon!

What did Sir Lancelot's mother say to him at bedtime?

"Knight, knight!"

What do you call a friendly pharaoh?

A chummy mummy!

Did you hear about the T. rex that ate a firework?

It was dinomite!

What did the executioner shout to the line of prisoners?

"Necks, please!"

Knock, knock.
Who's there?
Jester.
Jester who?
Jester wondering if you were at home!

What do you get if you cross a Roman emperor with a boa constrictor?

Julius Squeezer!

What was Queen Victoria's most treasured item of clothing?

Her reign-coat!

Say this three times, quickly!
Robin Hood robbed the rich of their riches until King Rich's return!

What creature hunted in prehistoric oceans?

Jurassic shark!

Did you hear about the Shakespearean actor who fell through the floor?

It was a just a stage he was going through!

What do you call a Roman emperor who has adventures?

An action Nero!

Why did cave people paint pictures of hippopotamuses?

They couldn't spell it!

HIPPYPIT TAMICE
HYPOPOT TYMOUTH
HAPPYPOTATOMAS

How did cavemen make fire with two sticks?

They made sure one was a match!

Why were the Dark Ages so confusing?

It was common to hear, "Good morning, good knight"!

What did Anne Boleyn's lady-in-waiting say on her wedding day?

"That man's not worth losing your head over!"

Knock, knock.

Who's there?

Julius.

Julius who?

Julius, seize her! She took my wallet!

Riddle me this!

I'm a sea where Egyptian mummies like to swim. What am I?

The Dead Sea.

Did you hear about the queen whose eldest son disobeyed her?

She was having a bad heir day!

What was the prisoner doing in the medieval dungeon?

Just hanging!

Say this three times, quickly.

The Queen's birthday is the third Thursday of this month!

What does an executioner read in the morning?

The noose-paper!

Who said, "Cluck, cluck!" and conquered half the world?

Attila the Hen!

How did Noah navigate in the dark?

With floodlights!

Why did the archer decide to change his career?

He found his work too arrowing!

How did people tie their shoelaces in the Middle Ages?

With a longbow!

Say this three times, quickly.

On various voyages, vile Vikings revolted violently!

Why did the dragon spit out the court jester?

Because he tasted funny!

What sweet treat did cavemen like the best?

Spearmints!

Why did the cowboy choose his horse in broad daylight?

He didn't want a nightmare!

Why wouldn't the ancient Egyptian accept that his boat was sinking?

He was in de Nile!

Why did the hangman's wife ask for a divorce?

Her husband was a pain in the neck!

What kind of dinosaur can you ride in a rodeo?

A Bronco-saurus!

What was T. rex's lucky number?

Eight!

Riddle me this. People could catch me, but they couldn't throw me. What am I?

The plague.

Why is it no fun being an archeologist?

Your career is always in ruins!

What did the dragon say when it saw Sir Lancelot?

"Ugh, more canned food!"

Which Roman emperor was the coolest?

Julius Freezer!

Say this three times, quickly.

Sir Lancelot, please dance a lot! Thanks a lot.

Which knight was King Arthur's best bodyguard?

Sir Curity!

Nero: What time is it?

Servant: X past VII!

What kind of socks did pirates wear?

Arrr-gyle!

What letters are like a Roman emperor?

The "Cs" are!

How did Christopher Columbus get to college?

On a scholar-ship!

Who do archeologists invite to their parties?

Anyone they can dig up!

Which knight was King Arthur's best lookout?

Sir Veillance!

In which battle was Genghis Khan killed?

His last one!

Which animal discovered the Internet?

The beaver—it was the first to log on!

Which famous knight never won a battle?

Sir Endor!

What loses its head in the morning but gets it back at night?

A pillow!

9.99

What comes once in a minute, twice in a moment, but never in a thousand years?

The letter "m."

When did the Vikings make their raids?

During a plunder storm!

Why did everyone laugh at the cowboy?

He was always horsing around!

Did you hear about the mummy that lost its temper?

It flipped its lid!

Say this three times, quickly.

Caesar saw his sister sitting on a seesaw!

A Year of Laughter

Where do you find the best Easter egg jokes?

In a yolk book!

Say this three times, quickly!

Peter Piper picked a pile of perfect pumpkins!

How did Jack Frost break his leg at Christmas?

He fell off his icicle!

When does Christmas come before Thanksgiving?

In the dictionary!

Why do skunks love Valentine's Day?

Because they're scent-imental!

What monster plays tricks at Halloween?

Prankenstein!

Why was the Thanksgiving turkey under arrest?

For fowl play!

How do you fix a jack-o'-lantern?

With a pumpkin patch!

What did the Easter bunny say about the horror film?

That was hare-raising!

Knock, knock.

Who's there?

Howl.

Howl who?

How-long till you open the door?

What did the slobbery dog say to her owner on Valentine's Day?

I love you drooly, madly, deeply!

Why is it so cold at Christmas?

Because it's Decembrrrr!

How do you win the Easter race?

By beating all the eggs!

When is a good time for Santa to come down the chimney?

Anytime!

Why was Santa's little helper shy?

He had low elf-esteem!

Which of Santa's reindeers was always impolite?

RUDE-olph!

How does the Easter bunny stay fit?

Eggs-ercise!

Knock, Knock.

Who's there?

Mary.

Mary who?

Mary Christmas!

What do you shout when Santa takes the roll call?

"Present!"

How do you start a Santa race?

On your marks, get set, ho ho ho!

Knock, Knock.

Who's there?

Abby.

Abby who?

Abby New Year!

Did you hear the one about the broken egg?

It will crack you up!

What should you wear to Thanksgiving dinner?

A har-vest!

Did you hear the story about the giant pumpkin pie?

It's a hard one to swallow …

Riddle me this!

If fruit comes from a fruit tree, where does turkey come from?

A poul-tree!

Why does Santa Claus enjoy being in the garden?

Because he likes to ho, ho, ho!

What do you get if you cross an apple with a Christmas tree?

A pineapple!

Why did the turkey want to join a band?

Because he already had the drumsticks!

What happened when the snow woman got angry at the snowman?

She gave him the cold shoulder!

THE GOBBLERS

Which ride do ghosts enjoy at Halloween?

The roller ghoster!

What did the magnet say to his girlfriend on Valentine's Day?

"You're very attractive!"

What did the Thanksgiving turkey say when it saw the farmer?

"Quack, quack!"

What birds write the most Christmas cards?

Pen-guins!

What do reindeer hang on their Christmas trees?

Horn-aments!

What do you get when you cross Santa Claus and Sherlock Holmes?

Santa Clues!

What do snowmen sing to Santa on his birthday?

"Freeze a jolly good fellow!"

What did Adam say to his wife the night before Christmas?

"It's Christmas, Eve!"

Say this three times, quickly!

Every Easter, Esther ate her eggs extremely eagerly!

What is impossible to pass at Christmas?

The Three Wide Men!

What did the sheep say to the shepherds at Christmas?

"Seasons bleatings!"

What do birds do on Halloween?

They go trick-or-tweeting!

What do you call a line of Easter rabbits who've been waiting in the sun too long?

Hot cross bunnies!

What goes "Oh, oh, oh!" at Christmas?

Santa walking backward!

What did the rabbits do after they got married?

They went on their bunny moon!

What kind of ball doesn't bounce?

A snowball!

Riddle me this! I have no hinge, door, or lid, but inside me, golden treasure is hidden. What am I?

An egg.

Why couldn't the elf work in Santa's toyshop?

He had tinsel-itis!

If Santa travels in a sleigh, what do his elves travel in?

A minivan!

Riddle me this! What always comes at the beginning of a parade?

The letter "p."

How many elves does it take to change a light bulb?

Ten—one to change the bulb and nine to stand on each other's shoulders!

What song does a bull sing on Valentine's Day?

"When I fall in love, it will be for heifer!"

What do you call a female elf?

A shelf!

How long should an elf's legs be?

Just long enough to reach the ground!

What did Santa say when he first sighted America?

"Land ho, ho, ho!"

What do you call Santa when he's asleep?

Santa Pause!

Say this three times, quickly. Eleven elves licked eleven lemon lollipops!

What kind of insect hates Christmas?

A bah humbug!

Where do you find the most famous mistletoe?

Holly-wood!

Where do the elves go to dance?

A snowball!

Why was the chicken in a fluster?

Because she'd mislaid her eggs!

What is different about the Christmas alphabet?

It has no "L"!

What kind of Easter eggs do aliens have?

Eggs-traterrestrial ones!

What does Jack Frost eat for breakfast?

Ice crispies!

How does the Easter bunny travel?

By hareplane!

What kind of music does the Easter bunny listen to?

Hip-hop!

Did you hear about the lazy skeleton? It was bone idle!

Say this three times, quickly.

Seven slippery snowmen slide silently southward!

What do you call it when chicks eat outdoors?

A peck-nic!

Who visits mermaids at Easter?

The oyster bunny!

What did the Cyclops write in his Valentine card?

"You're the one eye adore!"

Did you hear about the magnets that broke up?

They were poles apart!

Which TV show does the Easter bunny like best?

Who Wants to Be a Million-Hare.

What do you call someone who steals gift wrap from the rich and gives it to the poor?

Ribbon Hood!

What is it called if you're afraid of Christmas?

Santa Claus-trophobia!

What do snowmen like to do after Christmas?

Chill out!

How can you send a letter to the Easter bunny?

By hare mail!

What do snowmen eat for breakfast?

Frosted flakes!

What did the Python say to his girlfriend on Valentine's day?

"I've got a crush on you!"

What did one snowman say to the other?

"Can you smell carrots?"

Did you hear about the stupid vampire?

He was a real sucker!

What kind of flowers are no good for Valentine's Day?

Cauliflowers!

Knock, knock.
Who's there?
Owl.
Owl who?
Owl always love you, Valentine!

What did the farmer give his wife on Valentine's Day?

Hogs and kisses!

What did the gymnast say to her Valentine?

"I'm heels over head in love with you!"

What did Mrs. Claus say to Santa as she peered into the sky?

"Looks like rain deer!"

Why did the Easter bunny pull out of the marathon?

He was eggs-hausted!

Why is Santa so good at karate?

Because he has a black belt!

What kind of food is good for Valentine's Day?

A hearty meal!

Who is never hungry at Christmas?

A turkey, because he's always stuffed!

Who brings little crabs presents at Christmas?

Sandy Claws!

What does a nearsighted ghost need?

Spook-tacles!

What do you call a snowman in summer?

Puddle!

Riddle me this!

When Santa leaves the North Pole on Christmas Eve, in what direction does he travel?

South, because it is south in any direction from the North Pole.

What do Easter bunnies say to each other at Christmas?

"I wish you a Merry Christmas and a Hoppy New Year!"

What did the snail write in the Valentine's card?

"Be my Valen-slime!"

What is red and white and runs across the African plains?

A Santa-lope!

What always comes at the end of Christmas dinner?

The letter "r."

Knock, knock.

Who's there?

Howard.

Howard who?

Howard you like to be my Valentine?

How did the sheep propose to his girlfriend?

"Will ewe be my wife?"

What carol is sung in the desert?

O Cam-el Ye Faithful!

What did the rabbit say to the policeman when he knocked on his door?

I want to see your search warren!

How do you upset a reindeer?

Make an off-the-hoof remark!

What's the best kind of Christmas present?

A broken drum, because you just can't beat it!

What do ghosts name their teddy bears?

Winnie-the-Boo!

Which car do rabbits like best?

Any kind, as long as it's a hutchback!

What do ghouls put on their bagels?

Scream cheese!

Who has fangs and webbed feet?

Count Quackula!

What did one Easter egg say to the other?

"Heard any good yolks recently?"

Where does Easter come before Valentine's Day?

In the dictionary!

Who is Jack Frost's best-loved aunt?

Aunt Arctica!

How do you catch the Easter bunny?

Hide in the bushes, and make a noise like a carrot!

Knock, knock.

Who's there?

Harvey.

Harvey who?

Harvey happy Easter!

Why did Santa get a parking ticket?

He left his sleigh in a snow-parking zone!

What do you call a bunch of rabbits marching backward?

A receding hareline!

Why did Rudolph do so well at school?

Because he nose a lot and is very bright!

What do you call a Christmas tree with a really big nose?

Pine-ochio!

Who gives presents to baby sharks?

Santa Jaws!

What do snowmen wear on their heads?

Snowcaps!

What carol does Tarzan sing at Christmas?

Jungle Bells!

Why did the tortoises get married?

Because they were turtle-y in love!

How does Good King Wenceslas like his pizza?

Deep-pan, crisp, and even!

Say this three times, quickly.

How many deer would a reindeer rain, if a reindeer could rain deer?

Why are graveyards so noisy?

Because of all the coffin!

What do angry rodents send each other at Christmas?

Cross-mouse cards!

How does the Easter bunny travel home?

With United Hareways!